Pronunciation Guide for the Lectionary

A Comprehensive Resource for Proclaimers of the Word

Second Edition

Compiled by
Michael R. Prendergast,
Susan E. Myers, and
Timothy M. Milinovich

LITURGY
TRAINING
PUBLICATIONS

PRONUNCIATION GUIDE FOR THE LECTIONARY: A COMPREHENSIVE RESOURCE FOR PROCLAIMERS OF THE WORD, SECOND EDITION © 2017 Archdiocese of Chicago: Liturgy Training Publications, 3949 South Racine Avenue, Chicago, IL 60609; 800-933-1800, fax 800-933-7094, e-mail orders@ltp.org, website www.LTP.org. All rights reserved.

Editor, Lorie Simmons; production editor, Víctor R. Pérez; designer/production artist, Luis Leal; cover photo, John Zich.

Printed in the United States of America.

21   20   19   18   17   1   2   3   4   5

Library of Congress Control Number: 2017946205

ISBN 978-1-61671-374-4

PROGL2

Introduction

All ministers of the Word are called to hone their skills in the art of proclaiming God's Word and thus "speak to the weary / a word that will rouse them" (Isaiah 50:4). Whether in a cathedral, church, chapel, or outdoor arena, the creative, effective, and enduring Word of God has nourished the hearts of countless Catholics whenever priests, deacons, or other ministers of the Word have skillfully brought the texts of the Lectionary to life.

The Constitution on the Sacred Liturgy (*Sacrosanctum Concilium* [SC]), the first document promulgated by the Second Vatican Council, stresses the importance of God's Word in the life of the faithful: "They should be instructed by God's word and be nourished at the table of the Lord's body" (SC, 48). It goes on to say that the two parts of the Mass at which the people are instructed and nourished, "namely, the liturgy of the word and the liturgy of the eucharist, are so closely connected with each other that they form but one single act of worship" (56).

The Council Fathers expressed this unity in a striking image—"the one table of the word of God and the Body of Christ." They explained, "The church has always venerated the divine scriptures as it has venerated the Body of the Lord, in that it never ceases, above all in the sacred liturgy, to partake of the bread of life and to offer it to the faithful from the one table of the word of God and the Body of Christ" (Dogmatic Constitution on Divine Revelation [*Dei Verbum*, 21]).

The Word of God is one of the four ways in which Christ is present in the liturgy. In addition to the priest, the bread and wine that are transformed into the body and blood of Christ, and the gathered assembly, "[Christ] is present in his word since it is he himself who speaks when the holy Scriptures are read in Church" (SC, 7).

And so in the Word of God we find not simply history and inspiring stories, but rather, a living, dynamic reality in the life of the Church. In the Liturgy of the Word, we hear the record of God's saving work in the lives of the people whom God has chosen. These are stories told for a thousand generations, and they reinforce our identity as members of a community spanning time and space.

The remarkable relationship of Israel with its God required the people to be in constant communication, responding to God's Word. These responses were frank and assertive as well as worshipful and devout. Over time, they took on a formal character and became what we now call psalms. As the writers of the New Testament wrote their memories of Christ and his teachings, they read the psalms, stories, and prophecies of the Old Testament through the lens of Jesus Christ, handing on to Christians new interpretations of the ancient writings.

We know that these stories and songs, while based on history and tradition, are also in some mysterious way about us in our own time. And so we share with those who went before us a common heritage. Hearing the stories when we gather for liturgy reminds us of what God has done for his people in the past and what we can expect in the future. In addition, the stories give us the symbolic language that helps us understand God's presence in the midst of our lives.

Humans have known God through his Word, and also through his mighty deeds. In fact, the Hebrew word for "word" is *dabar,* and it means "deed" or "action" as well as "word." Seasoned proclaimers understand that the Word bristles with God's action and presence, and they work to proclaim the Word so that members of the assembly can experience that living presence. By becoming a transparent channel for the Word, proclaimers allow God's holy people to enter into communion with the God of love.

This pronunciation guide is intended especially for ministers of the Word who proclaim at Mass. It includes words from the *Lectionary for Mass*—Sundays, weekdays, and ritual Masses. As well as words from the Scripture, it includes names of saints and blesseds (for both the United States and Canada) and Latin words in the Lectionary's headings that may be needed by masters of ceremonies or presiders.

The ministry of proclaiming the Word of God requires skill and knowledge. Your training and the very task of preparing and proclaiming forms you and helps to make you worthy of the awesome responsibility entrusted to you. This guide will provide some essential, practical help.

Your preparation for proclaiming God's Word begins in private or in a small group as you read and meditate upon the selection you will share with your community. Read the passage in its biblical context to see what precedes and follows the verses you will proclaim. Find more on the history and meaning of your passage in a commentary or workbook designed for the purpose. Try to become part of the story or imagine yourself as a recipient of the message given. Don't despair if at first the passage is not clear or if the practices or attitudes seem foreign to you. What is important is that you are willing to learn what God is communicating. Reflect on it; pray about it.

Reading the text out loud is an important way to reflect on it. As you listen to your voice working on various tones, stresses, phrasings, volumes, and pauses, you will develop insights about how to convey meaning. Try different possibilities until you find what works best.

Be certain that you know how to pronounce *every word*. Although pronunciation may seem like a small detail, it is crucial for competent proclamation. Listeners should be able to easily recognize the words you proclaim. Even one inaccurate pronunciation can confuse listeners and prevent them from understanding the entire passage. At the least, mispronunciations are distracting and can mar the dignity of the proclamation. Finally, not being sure about how to pronounce the words in your reading can rob you of the confidence and calm that are so necessary for good proclamation.

Plan your phrasing and know when you will pause, when you will raise your voice, and when you will speak softly. Read the passage aloud repeatedly until you feel that you are ready. If possible, ask someone to listen to your proclamation and give you feedback.

When it is time for you to proclaim, take a deep breath. Move and speak slowly and clearly, enunciating every word. It may seem as though you are reading too slowly or are adding too much emphasis and inflection, but your listeners will find that helpful. In whatever you do, remain calm, dignified, and confident. If you stumble over a term, restate it correctly, then move on without drawing attention to the error. To present the divine Word effectively, you must have faith in your abilities and, at the same time, you must step back and allow God to work through you. Be humble, yet confident.

This guide focuses on words and phrases that may be unfamiliar or easily confused with other words. It is not meant to be exhaustive. Alternative pronunciations are sometimes provided since there may be several legitimate ways to render a name from the original Aramaic, Hebrew, Greek, or Latin into English. For biblical terms, in many cases this book follows *The HarperCollins Bible Pronunciation Guide* by William O. Walker Jr. with the Society of Biblical Literature, 1989. Names of saints are listed in their complete form, arranged alphabetically by the first name. This guide capitalizes some nouns that are capitalized in the Lectionary but may not be capitalized in normal use.

This resource tries to use the simplest means to indicate pronunciations. The following General Principles and Key show you how to interpret the pronunciations given.

General Principles

1. Consonants in English are straightforward. The letter B always represents the sound B, D is D, and so on.

2. Vowels are more complicated:

   Long I sound (kite or ice) is represented by ī or Ī.

   Long A (skate, pray) is represented by ay.

   Long E (beam, marine) is represented by ee.

   Long O (boat, coat) is represented by oh.

   Long U (tune, cute) is represented by oo or yoo.

   Short A (cat), E (bed), I (slim), and O (dot) are represented by a, e, i, and o—except in an unstressed syllable of a multi-syllable word, when E and I are signified by eh and ih.

   Short U (cup) is represented by uh.

3. An asterisk (*) indicates the schwa sound, as in the last syllable of the word "stable."

4. The letters OO and TH can each be pronounced in two ways (as in cool or book; thin or they); underlining differentiates between the two sounds.

5. Stress is indicated by the capitalization of the stressed syllable in words of more than one syllable.

Pronunciation Key

Capitalization indicates stressed syllable(s).

bait = bayt

cat = kat

sang = sang

father = FAH-<u>th</u>er

care = kayr

paw = paw

jar = jahr

easy = EE-zee

her = her

let = let

queen = kween

delude = deh-L<u>OO</u>D

when = hwen

ice = īs

if = if

finesse = fih-NES

thin = thin

vision = VIZH-*n

ship = ship

sir = ser

gloat = gloht

cot = kot

noise = noyz

poison = POY-z*n

plow = plow

although = awl-<u>TH</u>OH

church = cherch

fun = fuhn

fur = fer

flute = fl<u>oo</u>t

foot = foot

Comments and additions welcome: progl@ltp.org.

A

A ("A reading from . . .")	uh (<u>not</u> ay)
Aaron	AYR-uhn
Abana	AB-uh-nuh
abandon	uh-BAN-duhn
abated	uh-BAY-t*d
Abba	AH-bah
abbess	AB-uhs
abbot	AB-uht
Abednego	uh-BED-nih-goh
Abel	AY-b*l
Abel-meholah	AY-b*l muh-HOH-lah
Abiathar	uh-BĪ-uh-thahr
Abiel	AY-bee-el
Abijah	uh-BĪ-juh
Abilene	ab-uh-LEE-nee
Abinadab	uh-BIN-uh-dab
Abishai	uh-BĪ-shī
Abiud	uh-BĪ-uhd
abjection	ab-JEK-shun
Abner	AB-nehr
abolish	uh-BAWL-ihsh
abominable	uh-BAWM-nuh-b*l
abomination	uh-baw-muh-NAY-sh*n
Abraham	AY-bruh-ham
Abram	AY-br*m
Absalom	AB-suh-luhm
absurdity	uhb-SER-dih-tee or uhb-ZER-dih-tee
abundant	uh-BUHN-d*nt

abyss	uh-BIS
acclaim	uh-KLAYM
accompaniment	uh-KUHM-p*-nee-m*nt
accomplish	uh-KOM-plihsh
accord	uh-KOHRD
accordance	uh-KOHRD-*ns
accursed	uh-KERST or uh-KER-sihd
accusation	ak-yoo-ZAY-shuhn
accuse	uh-KYOOZ
Achaia	uh-KAY-yuh or uh-KEE-uh
Achilleus (Saint)	uh-KIL-ee-uhs
Achim	AY-kihm
Achor	AY-kohr
acknowledge	ak-NAW-ludj
acolytes	AK-oh-lītz
acquire	uh-KWĪR
acquittal	uh-KWIT-*l
Acts	akts
Adalbert (Saint)	AD-*l-behrt
Adam	AD-*m
adder	AD-*r
Addi	AD-ī
adherence	ad-HEER-*ns
Admah	AD-mah
Admin	AD-mihn
administer	ad-MIN-ih-stehr
administrator	ad-MIN-ih-stray-tehr
admonish	ad-MON-ish
adorns	uh-DOHRNZ
adulterous	uh-DUHL-tehr-uhs

adultery	uh-DUHL-tehr-ee
adversary	AD-vehr-sayr-ee
adversity	ad-VER-sih-tee
Advocate (noun)	AD-vuh-k*t
Aeneas	ih-NEE-uhs
Aenon	EE-nuhn
affect (verb)	uh-FEKT
afflict	uh-FLIKT
Agag	AY-gag
Agatha (Saint)	AG-uh-thuh
Agnes (Saint)	AG-nuhs
Agrippa	uh-GRIP-uh
Ahab	AY-hab
Ahaz	AY-haz
Ahaziah	ay-huh-ZĪ-uh
Ahijah	uh-HĪ-juh
Ahikam	uh-HĪ-kuhm
Ahiqar	uh-HĪ-kahr
alabaster	AL-uh-bas-tehr
Albert the Great (Saint)	AL-behrt thuh grayt
Alexander	al-ihg-ZAN-dehr
Alexandria	al-ehg-ZAN-dree-uh
alien	AY-lee-uhn
allege	uh-LEJ
alleluia	ah-lay-LOO-yuh
allot	uh-LOT
allure	uh-LOOR
Almighty	ahl-MĪ-tee
alms	olmz or ahmz
aloes	AL-ohz

aloof	uh-LOOF
Aloysius Gonzaga (Saint)	al-oh-WISH-uhs guhn-ZAHG-uh or gahn-ZAHG-uh
Alpha	AL-fuh
Alphaeus	AL-fee-uhs
Alphonsus Liguori (Saint)	al-FON-suhs luh-GOHR-ee
Amalek	AM-uh-lehk
Amalekites	uh-MAL-uh-kītz
Amaziah	am-uh-ZĪ-uh
ambassador	am-BAS-uh-dehr or am-BAS-uh-dohr
Ambrose (Saint)	AM-brohz
amen	ah-MEN or ay-MEN
Aminadab	uh-MIN-uh-dab
Amittai	uh-MIT-ī
Amminadab	uh-MIN-uh-dab
Ammonites	AM-uh-nītz
Amorites	AM-ehr-ītz
Amos	AY-m*s
Amoz	AY-muhz
Ampliatus	am-plee-AY-tuhs
analogy	uh-NAL-uh-jee
Ananias	a-nuh-NĪ-uhs
Anathoth	AN-uh-thoth
ancestors	AN-sehs-t*rs
ancestral	an-SES-tr*l
ancient	AYN-chuhnt
André Bessette (Saint)	ahn-DRAY buh-SET
André Grasset (Blessed)	ahn-DRAY grah-SAY or AHN-dray GRAH-seht

Andrew (Saint)	AN-dr<u>oo</u>
Andrew Du~ng-Lac (Saint)	AN-dr<u>oo</u> duhn LAK
Andrew Kim Taegŏn (Saint)	AN-dr<u>oo</u> kim TAY-gon
Andronicus	an-DRAHN-uh-kuhs
Angela Merici (Saint)	AN-juh-luh muh-REE-chee or muh-REE-see
anguish	ANG-wihsh
Anna	AN-uh
Annas	AN-uhs
Anne (Saint)	an
Annunciation	uh-nuhn-see-AY-shuhn
anointing	uh-NOYN-tihng
Anselm (Saint)	AN-sehlm
Ansgar (Saint)	AN-skahr
Anthony (Saint)	AN-thuh-nee
Anthony Mary Claret (Saint)	AN-thuh-nee MAYR-ee KLAYR-uht
Anthony Mary Zaccaria (Saint)	AN-thuh-nee MAYR-ee zak-uh-RĪ-uh
Anthony of Padua (Saint)	AN-thuh-nee uhv PA-juh-wuh or PA-dy<u>oo</u>-wuh
antimony	AN-tih-moh-nee
Antioch	AN-tee-ahk
Antiochus	an-TĪ-uh-kuhs
anxiety	ang-ZĪ-eh-tee
anxious	ANGK-shuhs
Aoar	AY-oh-ahr
Aphek	AY-fehk
Aphiah	uh-FĪ-uh
Apollinaris	uh-pahl-ih-NAYR-uhs

Apollos	uh-POL-uhs
apostasy	uh-POS-tuh-see
Apostles	uh-POS-*lz
appeal	uh-PEEL
appearance	uh-PIR-uhnz
appetizing	AP-uh-tīz-ihng
Appius	AP-ee-uhs
apportion	uh-POHR-shuhn
approached	uh-PROHCH*D
apron	AY-pruhn
Aquila	AK-wih-luh
Arabah	AYR-uh-buh
Arabia	uh-RAY-bee-uh
Arabs	AYR-uhbz
Aram	AYR-uhm
Aramean	ayr-uh-MEE-uhn
Araunah	uh-RAH-nuh
arbitrate	AHR-bih-trayt
Archangel	AHRK-ayn-jihl
Archelaus	ahr-kuh-LAY-uhs
Areopagus	ayr-ee-OP-uh-guhs
argument	AHR-gyoo-m*nt
Arimathea	ayr-ih-muh-THEE-uh
arisen	uh-RIZ-uhn
ark	ahrk
armor	AHR-muhr
Arni	AHR-nī
Aroer	uh-ROH-uhr
aromatic	ayr-oh-MAT-ihk
Arphaxad	ahr-FAK-sad

arrest	uh-REST
arrogance	AYR-uh-g*ns
arrogant	AYR-uh-g*nt
Artaxerxes	ahr-tuh-ZUHRK-seez
artisan	AHR-tih-z*n
Asa	AY-suh
Asaph	AY-saf
ascend	uh-SEND
ashamed	uh-SHAYMD
Asher	ASH-ehr
Ashtaroth	ASH-tuh-roth
Asia	AY-zhuh
Asmodeus	az-moh-DEE-uhs
assemble	uh-SEM-b*l
Assumption	uh-SUMP-shuhn
assurance	uh-SHOOR-*ns
assuredly	uh-SHOOR-uhd-lee
Assyria	uh-SEER-ee-uh
Astarte	az-TAHR-tee
astonish	uh-STAHN-uhsh
astound	uh-STOWND
astray	uh-STRAY
astrologers	uh-STRAHL-uh-jehrz
Athaliah	ath-uh-L$\bar{\text{I}}$-uh
Athanasius (Saint)	ath-uh-NAY-shee-uhs or ath-uh-NAY-shuhs or ath-uh-NAY-zhee-uhs or ath-uh NAY-zhuhs
Athens	ATH-uhnz
Athenian	uh-THEE-nee-uhn
atonement	uh-TOHN-m*nt

attain	uh-TAYN
Attalia	at-uh-LĪ-uh
attempt	uh-TEMPT
attendant	uh-TEN-duhnt
attentive	uh-TENT-t*v
attire	uh-TĪ-*hr
Augustine (Saint)	uh-GUHS-tihn or AH-guhs-teen
Augustine of Canterbury (Saint)	uh-GUHS-tihn or AH-guhs-teen uhv CAN-ter-buhr-ee
Augustine Zhao Rong (Saint)	uh-GUHS-tihn zhow-RONG
Augustus	aw-GUHS-tuhs
aura	AHR-uh
authority	uh-THOHR-ih-tee
avarice	AV-uh-rihs
avenge	uh-VENJ
avert	uh-VERT
Avni	AHV-nee
Azariah	az-uh-RĪ-uh
Azor	AY-zohr
Azotus	uh-ZOH-tuhs

B

Baal	BAY-uhl or bah-AHL
Baal-shalishah	BAY-uhl SHAHL-ih-shuh or BAH-uhl SHAHL-ih-shuh
Baasha	BAY-uh-shuh
Babel	BAY-b*l or BAB-*l
Babylon	BAB-ih-luhn

Babylonian	bab-uh-LOH-nee-uhn
Bahurim	buh-HYOOR-ihm
Balaam	BAY-luhm
Balamon	BAL-uh-muhn
bald	bahld
balm	bahlm
banquet	BAN-kwuht
Baptist	BAP-tihst
baptize	bap-TĪZ or BAP-tiz
Baptizer	bap-TĪ-zer
Barabbas	buh-RAB-uhs
barbarian	bahr-BAYR-ee-uhn
barbarous	BAHR-buhr-uhs
Barnabas (Saint)	BAHR-nuh-buhs
barren	BAYR-ehn
barricade	BAYR-ih-kayd
Barsabbas	bahr-SAH-buhs or bahr-SAB-uhs
Bartholomew (Saint)	bahr-THAHL-uh-myoo
Bartimaeus	bahr-tih-MAY-uhs or bahr-tih-MEE-uhs
Baruch	buh-ROOK
Bashan	BAY-shuhn
Basil the Great, (Saint)	BAY-zuhl or BA-zuhl
basilica	buh-SIL-ih-kuh
bathe	bayth
Bathsheba	bath-SHEE-buh
batten	BA-tehn
beam	beem
bearing	BAYR-ihng
beast	beest

B

Bede the Venerable (Saint)	BEED thuh VEN-er-uh-b*l
Beelzebul	bee-EL-zeh-buhl
beggar	BEG-*r
begotten	bee-GAW-t*n
beloved (noun)	bee-LUHV-uhd or buh-LUHV-uhd
Belshazzar	behl-SHAZ-uhr
Benedict (Saint)	BEN-uh-dihkt
benefactor	BEN-eh-fak-tehr
beneficent	buh-NEF-ih-suhnt
benefits	BEN-uh-fihtz
Benjamin	BEN-juh-muhn
Benjaminite	BEN-juh-muhn-īt
bereft	beh-REFT
Bernard (Saint)	ber-NAHRD or BER-nehrd
Bernardine of Siena (Saint)	BERN-ahr-deen uhv see-EN-uh
Bernice	behr-NEES
bestow	bih-STOH
Bethany	BETH-uh-nee
Bethel	BETH-*l
Bethlehem	BETH-luh-hehm
Beth-peor	beth-PEE-ohr
Bethphage	BETH-fuh-jee
Bethsaida	beth-SAY-uh-duh
Bethulia	bih-TH<u>OO</u>-lee-uh
betray	bih-TRAY
betrothed	bih-TROH<u>THD</u>
bidding	BID-ing
bier	beer

billows	BIL-ohz
bishop	BISH-uhp
Bithynia	bih-THIN-ee-uh
bitten	BI-tehn
bitumen	bih-TYOO-m*n or bih-TOO-m*n or bīh-TYOO-m*n
blame	blaym
Blase (or Blaise; Saint)	blayz
blaspheme	blas-FEEM
blasphemy	BLAS-fuh-mee
bleat	bleet
blemish	BLE-mish
Boanerges	boh-uh-NUHR-jeez
boast	bohst
Boaz	BOH-az
Bonaventure (Saint)	BON-uh-vehn-tyuhr
Boniface (Saint)	BON-uh-fuhs
booths	boothz
Borromeo	bohr-oh-MAY-oh
bosom	BOO-zuhm or BOO-zuhm
boundaries	BOWN-dreez or BOWN-duh-reez
bouts	bowtz
bow (rainbow)	boh
bow (verb)	bow
braggart	BRAY-guhrt
brandish	BRAN-dihsh
brazier	BRAY-zher
breach	breech
Bridget of Sweden (Saint)	BRI-dj*t uhv SWEE-d*n

briers	BRĪ-ehrz
brigand	BRIG-*nd
bronze	brawnz
brow	brow
bruise	brooz
Bruno (Saint)	BROO-noh
buffets	BUF-ihts
bullock	BUL-uhk
burdensome	BUR-d*n-s*m
burial	BAYR-ee-uhl
bury	BAYR-ee

C

Caesar	SEE-zehr
Caesarea	sez-uh-REE-uh or see-zuh-REE-uh
Caiaphas	KAY-uh-fuhs or KĪ-uh-fuhs
Cain	kayn
Cajetan (Saint)	KA-juh-tuhn
calamity	kuh-LAM-ih-tee
Callistus (Saint)	kuh-LIS-tuhs
Camillus de Lellis (Saint)	kuh-MIL-uhs day LEL-uhs
Cana	KAY-nuh
Canaan	KAY-n*n
Canaanite	KAY-nuh-nīt
Cananean	kay-nuh-NEE-uhn
Candace	KAN-duh-see or kan-DAY-see
candidacy	KAN-dih-duh-see

Capernaum	kuh-PER-nee-*m or kuh-PER-nay-*m or kuh-PER-n*m
Cappadocia	kap-uh-DOH-shuh or kap-uh-DOH-shee-uh
caption	KAP-shuhn
captivate	KAP-tih-vayt
captivity	kap-TI-vih-tee
caravan	KAYR-uh-van
carbuncles	KAHR-bung-k*lz
carcass	KAHR-kuhs
Carians	KAYR-ee-uhnz
Carmel	KAHR-m*l
carnal	KAHR-n*l
carnelian	kahr-NEEL-yuhn
carousing	kuh-ROW-zing
Carpus	KAHR-puhs
Casimir (Saint)	KA-zih-meer
castles	KA-s*lz
cataracts	KAT-uh-raktz
catechist	KAT-uh-kihst
catechumen	kat-uh-KYOO-m*n
Catechumenate	kat-uh-KYOO-m*n-uht
Catherine de Saint-Augustin (Blessed)	*See* Catherine of Saint Augustine
Catherine of Alexandria (Saint)	KATH-rihn uhv al-eg-ZAN-dree-uh
Catherine of Saint Augustine (Blessed)	KATH-rihn uhv saynt-uh-GUHS-tin
Catherine of Siena (Saint)	KATH-rihn uhv see-EN-uh
caught	kawt

Cecilia (Saint)	suh-SEEL-yuh or suh-SEE-lee-uh
cedar	SEE-dehr
cenacle	SEN-uh-k*l
Cenchreae	SEN-kruh-ee or SEN-kree-ay
censure	SEN-shuhr
centurion	sen-TOOR-ee-uhn or sen-TYOOR-ee-uhn
Cephas	SEE-fuhs
cereal	SEER-ee-uhl
ceremonial	sayr-uh-MOH-nee-uhl
certifies	SER-tih-fīz
chaff	chaf
Chaldeans	kal-DEE-uhnz or kahl-DEE-uhnz
chalice	CHA-luhs
chamber	CHAYM-behr
champion	CHAM-pee-uhn
charcoal	CHAHR-kohl
charioteer	chayr-ee-uh-TEER
charlatan	SHAHR-luh-t*n
Charles Borromeo (Saint)	chahrlz bohr-oh-MAY-oh
Charles Lwanga (Saint)	chahrlz luh-WAHN-guh
chasm	KAZ-*m
chastise	chas-TĪZ
Chebar	KEE-bahr
Chemosh	KEE-mosh
cherish	CHAYR-ihsh
Cherith	KER-ihth or KEE-rihth
cherubim	CHAYR-uh-bihm

chide	chīd
Chilion	KIL-ee-uhn
chisel	CHIZ-uhl
Chislev	KIZ-lehv
Chloe	KLOH-ee
Chorazin	koh-RAY-zihn
Christ	krīst
Christian	KRIS-chuhn
Christopher Magallanes (Saint)	KRIS-tuh-fehr mah-gahl-YAH-nehs
Chronicles	KRAH-nih-k*ls
Chuza	KYOO-zuh
Cilicia	suh-LISH-ee-uh
circulate	SER-kyoo-layt
circumcise	SER-kuhm-sīz
circumcision	sehr-kuhm-SI-zhuhn
circumstance	SER-kuhm-stants
cistern	SIS-tehrn
citizen	SI-tuh-zuhn
civil	SI-v*l
clamorous	KLAM-ehr-uhs
clan	klan
Clare (Saint)	klayr
Claudius	CLAW-dee-uhs
cleansed	klenzd
cleft	klehft
clemency	KLEM-*n-see
Clement (Saint)	KLEM-*nt
Cleopas	KLEE-oh-puhs
Clopas	KLOH-puhs
cloth (noun)	klawth

clothe (verb)	klohth
cluster	KLUHS-tehr
cohort	KOH-hohrt
collapse	kuh-LAPS
collect (verb)	kuh-LEHKT
Colossians	kuh-LOSH-uhnz
Columban (Saint)	kuh-LUHM-b*n
column	KOL-uhm
comeliness	KUHM-lee-n*s
comfortable	KUHM-fehr-tuh-b*l
commend	kuh-MEND
commemoration	kuh-mehm-uhr-AY-shuhn
commendation	kah-mehn-DAY-shuhn
commit	kuh-MIT
communal	kuh-MYOON-*l or KOM-yoo-n*l
companion	kuhm-PAN-yuhn
compassionate	kuhm-PASH-uhn-uht
compel	kuhm-PEL
competent	KOM-puh-t*nt
complacent	kuhm-PLAY-s*nt
concealing	kuhn-SEEL-ing
conceit	kuhn-SEET
conceive	kuhn-SEEV
Conception	kuhn-SEP-shuhn
concern	kuhn-SERN
condemn	kuhn-DEM
condemnation	kon-d*m-NAY-shuhn
confer	kuhn-FER
conferral	kuhn-FER-*l
confinement	kuhn-FĪN-m*nt

confront	kuhn-FRUHNT
confusion	kuhn-FYOO-shuhn
congeal	kuhn-JEEL
congregation	kong-greh-GAY-shuhn
congress	KON-grehs
conquer	KONG-kuhr
conscience	KON-shuhns
consecrate	KON-suh-krayt
consent	kuhn-SENT
consequently	KON-suh-kwent-lee
consolation	kon-suh-LAY-shuhn
console	kuhn-SOHL
constancy	KON-stuhn-see
constellation	kon-stuh-LAY-shuhn
constrain	kuhn-STRAYN
construct	kuhn-STUHKT
consult	kuhn-SUHLT
contemplate	KON-tuhm-playt
contemptible	kuhn-TEMP-tuh-b*l
content (adjective)	kuhn-TENT
contention	k*n-TEN-shuhn
contradict	kahn-truh-DICT
contrary	KAHN-trayr-ee
contributor	kuhn-TRIB-yoo-tehr
contrite	kuhn-TRĪT
contrive	kuhn-TRĪV
controversy	KON-truh-vehr-see
converse	kuhn-VERS
conversion	kuhn-VER-zhuhn
convince	kuhn-VINS

Corinth	KOHR-ihnth
Corinthians	kohr-IN-thee-uhnz
Cornelius (Saint)	kohr-NEEL-yuhs
corpse	kohrps
corrode	kuh-ROHD
corruptible	kohr-RUPT-uh-b*l
Cosam	KOH-suhm
Cosmas (Saint)	KAHZ-muhs
cosmos	KAHS-mohs
counsel	COWN-suhl
countenance	KOWN-tuh-n*ns
courageous	kehr-RAY-juhs
covenant	KUHV-eh-n*nt
covet	KUHV-iht
cowardice	KOW-ehr-dihs
cowardly	KOW-ehrd-lee
crags	kraygz
crave	krayv
Crescens	KRES-uhns
Cretans	KREE-tuhns
crevices	KRE-vihs-*s
crimson	KRIM-zuhn
cripple	KRI-p*l
crucifixion	kroo-sih-FIK-shuhn
crucify	KROO-sih-fī
cultivation	kuhl-tih-VAY-shuhn
cumin	KYOO-muhn
cunning	CUHN-ing
curds	kerds
cure	kyoor

curse	kuhrs
cushion	koosh-*n
Cushite	KOOSH-īt
custody	KUHS-tih-dee
cymbal	SIM-buhl
Cyprian (Saint)	SIP-ree-uhn
Cypriot	SIP-ree-uht
Cyprus	SĪ-pruhs
Cyrene	sī-REEN or sī-REE-nee
Cyrenian	sī-REE-nee-uhn
Cyril (Saint)	SEER-*l
Cyril of Alexandria (Saint)	SEER-*l uhv al-eg-ZAN-dree-uh
Cyril of Jerusalem (Saint)	SEER-*l uhv juh-ROO-suh-lem
Cyrus	SĪ-ruhs

D

Dalmanutha	dal-muh-NOO-thuh
Damaris	DAM-uh-rihs
Damascus	duh-MAS-kuhs
Damasus (Saint)	DAM-uh-suhs
Damian (Saint)	DAY-mee-uhn
Damien Joseph de Veuster of Moloka'i (Saint)	DAY-mee-uhn zhoh-SEF d* vehs-TAYR uhv MOL-uh-kī
dandle	DAN-d*l
Daniel	DAN-yuhl
Danites	DAN-ītz
David	DAY-vihd
deacon	DEE-kuhn
deaf	def

debase	dih-BAYS
debauchery	dih-BAW-chuh-ree
debt	det
debtor	DET-ehr
Decapolis	dih-KAP-uh-lis
deceit	dih-SEET
decision	dih-SI-zhuhn
decrease (verb)	dih-KREES
decree	dih-KREE
decrepit	dih-KREP-it
dedication	ded-ih-KAY-shuhn
defense	dih-FENS
deference	DEF-uh-rehns
defraud	dih-FRAWD
deity	DEE-ih-tee
delegation	dehl-eh-GAY-shuhn
deliberations	dih-lihb-uh-RAY-shuhnz
deluge	DEL-yooj or DEL-yoozh
Demas	DEE-muhs
demon	DEE-muhn
demoniacs	dih-MON-ee-aks
demoralize	dih-MOHR-uhl-iz
denarii	dih-NAHR-ee-ī
denarius	dih-NAHR-ee-uhs
Denis (Saint)	DEN-ihs
denounce	dih-NOWNS
deny	dee-NĪ
Derbe	DER-bee
deride	dih-RĪD
derive	dih-RĪV

27

descendant	dih-SEN-d*nt
desert (noun)	DEZ-ehrt
desert (verb)	dih-ZERT
deserve	dih-ZERV
design	dih-ZĪN
desolate	DES-uh-liht
desolation	dehs-oh-LAY-shuhn
despise	dih-SPĪZ
despoiler	dih-SPOY-l*r
despondent	dih-SPAHN-d*nt
destine	DES-tihn
destiny	DES-tih-nee
detest	dih-TEST
destitute	DES-tih-t<u>oo</u>t
destruction	dih-STRUHK-shuhn
Deuteronomy	d<u>oo</u>-ter-AH-nuh-mee or dy<u>oo</u>-ter-AH-nuh-mee
Devil	DEV-*l
devious	DEE-vee-uhs
devoid	dih-VOYD
devote	dih-VOHT
devour	dih-VOWR
devout	dih-VOWT
dew	d<u>oo</u>
diaconate	dee-AK-uh-nuht
diadem	DĪ-uh-dem
dictate (noun)	DIK-tayt
Didymus	DID-uh-muhs
dignitary	DIG-nih-tayr-ee
diligent	DIL-ih-j*nt
Dina Bélanger (Blessed)	DEE-nuh bay-lahn-ZHAY

Dionysius	dī-uh-NĪ-suhs
Dioscuri	dī-OS-kuh-ree
dire	dīr
discern	dih-SERN
discernment	dih-SERN-m*nt
disciple	dih-SĪ-p*l
discipline	DIS-ih-plihn
discord	DIS-kohrd
disdain	dihs-DAYN
disease	diz-EEZ
disembark	dihs-em-BAHRK
disgraced	dihs-GRAYS*D
disheveled	dih-SHEV-uhld
dislocate	DIS-loh-kayt or dihs-LOH-kayt
dismal	DIZ-muhl
dispense	dihs-PENS
disperse	dihs-PERS
dispossess	dihs-poh-ZES
dissension	dih-SEN-shuhn
dissipation	dihs-ih-PAY-shuhn
dissolute	DIS-uh-loot
dissolution	dihs-uh-LOO-shuhn
dissuade	dih-SWAYD
distinguish	dihs-TING-wish*d
distribute	dihs-TRI-byoot
distribution	dihs-tri-BYOO-shuhn
disturbance	dihs-TUHR-buhns
diverse	dih-VERS
divination	dih-vihn-AY-shuh
docile	DOS-*l

domination	dom-ih-NAY-shuhn
Dominic (Saint)	DOM-ih-nihk
dominion	doh-MIN-yuhn
Dorcas	DOHR-kuhs
Dothan	DOH-thuhn
dromedary	DROM-eh-dayr-ee
drought	drowt
dungeon	DUHN-juhn
duplicity	doo-PLIH-sih-tee
dwelt	dwehlt
dynasty	DĪ-nuh-stee

E

earnestness	ER-nuhst-n*s
Ebed-melech	ee-bihd-MEE-lihk
Ebenezer	ehb-uh-NEE-zuhr
Eber	EE-buhr
Ecclesiastes	ih-klee-zee-AS-teez
ecstasy	EK-stuh-see
Eden	EE-d*n
Edna	ED-nuh
Edom	EE-d*m
Egypt	EE-jihpt
Egyptians	ee-JIP-shuhnz
Elamites	EE-luh-mīts
Eldad	EL-dad
elder	EL-duhr
Eleazar	el-ee-AY-zehr
electrum	ih-LEK-truhm
elemental	ehl-uh-MEN-tuhl
Eli	EE-lī

Eli, Eli, lema sabachthani	ay-LEE, ay-LEE, luh-MAH sah-bahk-tah-nee
Eliab	ee-LĪ-uhb
Eliakim	ee-LĪ-uh-kihm
Eliam	ih-LĪ-uhm
Eliezer	el-ee-AY-zehr
Elihu	ih-LĪ-hyoo
Elijah	ee-LĪ-juh
Elim	EE-lihm
Elisha	ee-LI-shuh
Eliud	ee-LĪ-uhd
Elizabeth (Saint)	ee-LIZ-uh-behth
Elizabeth Ann Seton (Saint)	ee-LIZ-uh-behth an SEE-tuhn
Elizabeth of Hungary (Saint)	ee-LIZ-uh-behth uhv HUNG-uh-ree
Elizabeth of Portugal (Saint)	ee-LIZ-uh-behth uhv POHR-chih-guhl or POHR-tyoo-gahl
Elkanah	ehl-KAY-nah
Elmadam	ehl-MAY-duhm
Elnathan	ehl-NAY-thuhn
Eloi, Eloi, lema sabachthani	ehl-oh-ee, ehl-oh-ee, luh-MAH sah-bahk-tah-nee or ay-loh-ee
eloquence	EL-uh-kwens
elusive	ih-LOO-sihv
Elymais	ehl-uh-MAY-uhs
ember	EM-behr
embroider	ehm-BROY-dehr
emerald	EM-ehr-uhld

Émilie Tavernier-Gamelin (Blessed)	ay-mih-LEE ta-vehr-NYAY gam-uh-LAHN or EM-uh-lee ta-vehr-NIR GAM-ih-lihn
Emmanuel	ee-MAN-yoo-el
Emmaus	eh-MAY-uhs
encamp	ehn-KAMP
encompass	ehn-KUHM-puhs
encumbrance	ehn-KUHM-br*ns
endow	ehn-DOW
endurance	ehn-DOOR-*ns or ehn-DYOOR-*ns
enjoin	ehn-JOYN
enmity	EN-mih-tee
Enoch	EE-nuhk
enormous	ee-NOHR-muhs
Enos	EE-nuhs
enrapture	ehn-RAP-tyuhr
entail	ehn-TAYL
enticement	ehn-TĪS-m*nt
envelop (verb)	ehn-VEL-uhp
envious	EN-vee-uhs
envy	EN-vee
Epaenetus	ih-PEE-nuh-tuhs
Epaphras	EP-uh-fras
ephah	EE-fuh
Ephesians	ee-FEE-zhuhnz
Ephesus	EF-uh-suhs
Ephphatha	EF-uh-thuh
Ephraim	EE-fray-ihm or EF-r*m
Ephrathah	EF-ruh-thuh

Ephrem (Saint)	EF-ruhm
Epiphany	ih-PIF-uh-nee
equity	EK-wih-tee
Er	uhr
Esau	EE-saw
espouse	ehs-POWS
establish	ehs-TAB-lish
estate	ehs-TAYT
esteem	ehs-TEEM
Esther	ES-tehr
eternal	ee-TER-nuhl
Ethanim	ETH-uh-nihm
Ethiopian	ee-thee-OH-pee-uhn
Eucharist	YOO-kuh-rihst
Eugène de Mazenod (Saint)	oo-ZHEN d* ma-zeh-NOH or yoo-JEEN d* ma-zehn-AHD
Eunice	YOO-nuhs
eunuch	YOO-nuhk
Euphrates	yoo-FRAY-teez
Eusebius of Vercelli (Saint)	yoo-SEE-bee-uhs uhv vehr-CHEL-ee
evangelization	ee-VAN-j*l-ih-ZAY-shuhn
evidence	EV-uh-duhnts
evil	EE-vuhl
ewe	yoo
exalt	ehg-ZAHLT
exaltation	ehks-uhl-TAY-shuhn
excellency	EK-sehl-lehn-see
exception	ehk-SEP-shuhn
execution	ehk-suh-KYOO-shuhn

exercise	EK-sehr-sīz
exhaustion	ehg-ZAWS-chuhn
exhort	ehg-ZOHRT
exhortation	ehg-zohr-TAY-shuhn
exile	EG-zīl or EK-sīl
exist	ehg-ZIST
Exodus	EK-suh-duhs
expanse	ehk-SPANS
expiate	EK-spee-ayt
expiation	ehk-spee-AY-shuhn
exterminate	ehk-STER-min-ayt
extinguish	ehk-STING-gwish
extol	ehk-STOHL
extort	ehk-STOHRT
extortion	ehk-STOHR-shuhn
exult	ehg-ZUHLT
Ezekiel	ee-ZEE-kee-uhl
Ezra	EZ-ruh

F

Fabian (Saint)	FAY-bee-uhn
facade	fuh-SAHD
famine	FAM-ihn
famished	FAM-ihsht
Father	FAH-thehr
Fatima	FA-tih-muh
Felicity (Saint)	fuh-LIS-ih-tee
Felix (Saint)	FEE-lihx
fertile	FUHR-t*l
festal	FES-tuhl
Festus	FEST-uhs

fetter	FET-*r
Fidelis of Sigmaringen (Saint)	fih-DEL-lihs uhv zihg-MAHR-ing-*n
fidelity	fih-DEL-uh-tee or fī-DEL-uh-tee
fiend	feend
fierce	feers
figuratively	FIG-yehr-uh-tihv-lee
firmament	FER-muh-m*nt
flog	flog or flawg
foal	fohl
fodder	FOD-ehr
forbade	fohr-BAD or fohr-BAYD
forbearance	fohr-BAYR-*ns
foreign	FOHR-uhn
foreknowledge	FOHR-nahl-ihj
forfeit	FOHR-fuht
fornication	fohr-nih-KAY-shuhn
fowler's	FOW-lehrz
fragmentary	FRAG-m*n-tayr-ee
Frances of Rome (Saint)	FRAN-suhs uhv rohm
Frances Xavier Cabrini (Saint)	FRAN-suhs ZAY-vee-uhr kuh-BREE-nee
Francis de Sales (Saint)	FRAN-sihs duh SAYLZ
Francis of Assisi	FRAN-sihs uhv uh-SEEZ-ee
Francis of Paola (Saint)	FRAN-sihs uhv puh-OH-luh
Francis Xavier (Saint)	FRAN-sihs ZAY-vee-uhr
Francis Xavier Seelos (Blessed)	FRAN-sihs ZAY-vee-ehr SEE-lohs
François de Laval (Blessed)	fran-SWAH d* lah-VAL

frankincense	FRANG-kuhn-sehns
Frédéric Janssoone (Blessed)	fray-day-REEK zhahn-SOON or FRED-ehr-ihk jan-SOON
fugitive	FY<u>OO</u>-jih-tihv
fuller's lye	FUHL-ehrs lī
fullers' soap	FUHL-ehrs sohp
functionary	FUNK-shuhn-ayr-ee
furnace	FUHR-n*s
futile	FY<u>OO</u>-t*l

G

Gabbatha	GAB-uh-thuh
Gabriel (Saint)	GAY-bree-uhl
Gadarenes	GAD-uh-reenz
Galatia	guh-LAY-shuh or guh-LAY-shee-uh
Galatians	guh-LAY-shuhnz
Galilean	gal-ih-LEE-uhn
Galilee	GAL-ih-lee
gall	gawl
Gallio	GAL-ee-oh
Gamaliel	guh-MAY-lee-uhl
Gaza	GAH-zuh
Gedaliah	gehd-uh-LĪ-uh
Gehazi	geh-HAY-zī
Gehenna	geh-HEN-nah
genealogy	jee-nee-AL-uh-jee or jee-nee-OL-uh-jee
generation	jehn-ehr-AY-shuhn
generative	JEN-ehr-uh-tihv
Genesis	JEN-uh-sihs

Gennesaret	geh-NES-uh-reht
Gentiles	JEN-tīls
genuflect	JEN-yoo-flekt
genuineness	JEN-yoo-ihn-n*s
George (Saint)	johrj
Gera	GEE-ruh
Gerasenes	GER-uh-seenz
Gertrude (Saint)	GER-trood
gesture	GES-tyoor
Gethsemane	gehth-SEM-uh-nee
Gibeon	GIB-ee-uhn
Gideon	GID-ee-uhn
Gilead	GIL-ee-uhd
Gilgal	GIL-gahl
gird	gerd
Girgashites	GUHR-guh-shītz
gloat	gloht
glorify	GLOHR-ih-fī
glutton	GLUH-t*n
gnash	nash
gnat	nat
Golgotha	GAWL-guh-thuh
Gomorrah	guh-MOHR-ah
gong	gawng
gorges	GOHR-juhz
Goshen	GOH-shuhn
gouge	gowj
governor	GUV-ehr-nuhr
Gozan	GOH-zan
gracious	GRAY-shuhs

granary	GRAYN-uh-ree
grandeur	GRAN-j*r
Greek	greek
Gregory (VII, Saint)	GREG-uh-ree
Gregory the Great (Saint)	GREG-uh-ree thuh grayt
Gregory Nazianzen (Saint)	GREG-uh-ree na-see-AN-zuhn
grievances	GREE-v*n-suhz
grievous	GREE-vuhs
grudge	gruhdj
Guadalupe	gwah-duh-LOO-pay
Guardian	GAHR-dee-uhn
gymnasium	jihm-NAY-zee-uhm

H

Habakkuk	huh-BAK-kuhk or HAB-uh-kuhk
Hadadrimmon	hay-dad-RIM-uhn
Hades	HAY-deez
Hagar	HAY-gahr
Haggai	HAYG-ī
Halah	HAY-luh
hallelujah	ha-lay-LOO-yuh
hallowed	HAL-ohd
Ham	ham
Haman	HAY-muhn
Hananiah	han-uh-NĪ-uh
Hannah	HAN-uh
Haran	HAYR-uhn
harbor	HAHR-behr
hasten	HAY-suhn

hearth	hahrth
Hebrews	HEE-br<u>oo</u>z
Hebron	HEB-ruhn
Hedwig (Saint)	HED-wig
heifer	HEF-ehr
heir	ayr
Heli	HEE-lī
Hellenist	HEL-uh-nist
hemorrhage	HEM-ehr-rihj
henceforth	HENS-fohrth
Henry (Saint)	HEN-ree
heritage	HAYR-ih-tihj
Hermes	HUHR-meez
Herod	HAYR-uhd
Herodian	hehr-OH-dee-uhn
Hezekiah	hehz-eh-KĪ-uh
Hezron	HEZ-ruhn
Hilary (Saint)	HIL-uh-ree
Hilkiah	hil-KĪ-uh
hind	hīnd
Hippolytus (Saint)	hihp-PAW-lih-tuhs
hireling	HĪR-ling
Hittite	HIT-tīt
Hivites	HIH-vītz
hoarfrost	HOHR-frawst
hoist	hoyst
holies	HOH-leez
holocaust	HAHL-uh-kawst or HOH-luh-kawst
Holy Spirit	HOH-lee SPEER-iht
homage	OM-ihj or HOM-ihj

honor	ON-ehr
honorable	ON-ehr-uh-b*l
Hophni	HOF-nī
Horeb	HOHR-eb
hosanna	hoh-ZAH-nah
hosannah	hoh-ZAH-nah
Hosea	hoh-ZAY-uh
hostile	HAH-st*l
hostility	hah-STIL-uh-tee
hover	HUH-vehr
humble	HUM-b*l
humiliation	hyoo-mil-ee-AY-shuhn
humility	hyoo-MIL-ih-tee
Hungary	HUHN-guh-ree
Hur	her
hymn	him
hypocrite	HIP-uh-kriht
hyssop	HIS-uhp

I

Iconium	ī-KOH-nee-uhm
idly	ĪD-lee
idolatry	ī-DOL-uh-tree
Idumea	ih-djoo-MEE-uh
Ignatius of Antioch (Saint)	ihg-NAY-shee-uhs uhv AN-tee-ahk
Ignatius of Loyola (Saint)	ihg-NAY-shee-uhs uhv loy-OH-luh
illicit	ih-LIS-iht
Illyricum	ih-LIR-ih-kuhm
immaculate	ihm-MAK-yoo-luht

Immaculate Conception	ih-MAK-yoo-luht kuhn-SEP-shuhn
Immanuel	ihm-MAN-yoo-el
immense	ih-MENS
immerse	ih-MERS
imminent	IM-uh-nuhnt
immorality	ih-mohr-AL-ih-tee
immortal	ih-MOHR-t*l
immortality	ihm-ohr-TAL-ih-tee
immovable	ih-MOO-vuh-b*l
impartiality	ihm-pahr-shee-AL-ih-tee
impediment	ihm-PED-ih-m*nt
imperishability	ihm-payr-ih-shuh-BIL-ih-tee
imperishable	ihm-PAYR-ih-shuh-b*l
impiety	ihm-PĪ-eh-tee
impious	IM-pee-uhs
implore	ihm-PLOHR
impostor	ihm-PAH-st*r
imprisonment	ihm-PRIZ-uhn-m*nt
improvise	IM-pruh-vīz
impudence	IM-pyoo-d*ns
impudent	IM-pyoo-d*nt
inapproachable	ihn-uh-PROH-chuh-b*l
incense (verb)	ihn-SENS
incite	ihn-SĪT
incorruptibility	ihn-koh-ruhp-tuh-BIL-ih-tee
incorruptible	ihn-koh-RUHP-tuh-b*l
incorruption	ihn-koh-RUHP-shuhn

incredulous	ihn-KRED-yoo-luhs or ihn-KREJ-uh-luhs
incur	ihn-KUHR
incurable	ihn-KYUHR-uh-b*l
indescribable	ihn-dih-SKRĪB-uh-b*l
indulgence	ihn-DUHL-j*ns
industrious	ihn-DUHS-tree-uhs
inferior	ihn-FEER-ee-ehr
infirmity	ihn-FER-mih-tee
infuriate	ihn-FYOOR-ee-ayt
inhabited	ihn-HAB-ih-tuhd
inheritance	ihn-HAYR-ih-t*ns
iniquity	ihn-NIK-wih-tee
initiative	ihn-NISH-ee-uh-tihv or ihn-NISH-uh-tihv
Innocents	IN-uh-suhnts
innumerable	ih-NOO-mer-uh-b*l or ih-NYOO-mer-uh-b*l
inscrutable	ihn-SKROO-tuh-b*l
insistent	ihn-SIS-t*nt
insolence	IN-suh-l*ns
insult (noun)	IN-suhlt
insult (verb)	ihn-SUHLT
insurgents	ihn-SER-j*nts
insurrection	ihn-suh-REK-shuhn
integrity	ihn-TEG-rih-tee
intercede	ihn-tehr-SEED
intercession	ihn-tehr-SESH-uhn
interior	ihn-TEER-ee-uhr
interrogate	ihn-TAYR-uh-gayt
interrogation	ihn-tayr-uh-GAY-shuhn

intervene	ihn-tehr-VEEN
intoxicants	ihn-TOK-sih-k*nts
intrigue (verb)	ihn-TREEG
Irenaeus (Saint)	eer-uh-NAY-uhs
irreproachable	eer-rih-PROH-chuh-b*l
irrevocable	ih-REV-uh-kuh-b*l
irritable	EER-ih-tuh-b*l
Isaac	Ī-zik
Isaac Jogues (Saint)	Ī-zik johgz
Isaiah	ī-ZAY-uh
Iscariot	ih-SKAYR-ee-uht
Ishmael	ISH-may-uhl
Ishmaelites	ISH-may-uh-lītz
Isidore (Saint)	IZ-uh-dohr
isle	īl
Israel	IZ-ree-uhl or IZ-ray-uhl
Israelite	IZ-ree-uh-līt or IZ-ray-uh-līt
Ituraea	ih-too-REE-ah

J

jackal	JAK-uhl
Jacob	JAY-kuhb
Jairus	JĪ-ruhs or jay-Ī-ruhs
James (Saint)	jaymz
Jane Frances de Chantal (Saint)	jayn FRAN-suhs d* shan-TAHL
Jannai	JAN-ī
Januarius (Saint)	jan-yoo-AYR-ee-uhs
Jared	JAYR-ihd
jasper	JAS-pehr

Javan	JAY-vuhn
Jean de Brébeuf	*See* John de Brébeuf
Jebusites	JEB-yoo-sitz
Jechoniah	jek-oh-NĪ-uh
Jehoiachim	jih-HOI-uh-kim
Jehoiada	jih-HOI-uh-duh
Jehoshaphat	jeh-HOH-shuh-fat
Jehozadak	jih-HOH-zuh-dak
Jehu	JAY-hoo
Jephthah	JEF-thuh
Jeremiah	jayr-uh-MĪ-uh
Jericho	JAYR-ih-koh
Jeroboam	jer-uh-BOH-uhm
Jeroham	jih-ROH-ham
Jerome (Saint)	jehr-OHM
Jerome Emiliani (Saint)	jehr-OHM eh-mee-lee-AH-nee
Jerusalem	juh-ROO-suh-lehm or juh-ROO-zuh-lehm
Jesse	JES-ee
Jesus	JEE-zuhz or JEE-zuhs
Jesus'	JEE-zuhz or JEE-zuhs (not JEE-zuh-zuhz)
Jethro	JETH-roh
Jezreel	JEZ-ree-uhl
Joachim (Saint)	JOH-uh-kihm
Joakim	JOH-uh-kihm
Joanna	joh-AN-uh
Joash	JOH-ash
Job	johb
Joda	JOH-duh

Joel	JOH-*l
John (Saint)	jon
John (XXIII, Saint)	jon
John Baptist de la Salle (Saint)	jon BAP-tihst day luh-SAL or dee luh-SAL
John Bosco (Saint)	jon BAHS-koh
John Chrysostom (Saint)	jon KRIS-ihs-t*m or krihs-IS-t*m
John de Brébeuf (Saint)	jon d* BRAY-buhf
John Eudes (Saint)	jon yoodz
John Fisher (Saint)	jon FISH-ehr
John Kanty (Saint)	jon KAN-tee
John Leonardi (Saint)	jon lee-uh-NAHR-dee
John Mary Vianney	jon MAYR-ee vee-AH-nee
John Neumann (Saint) (Saint)	jon NOO-muhn
John of Capistrano (Saint)	jon uhv kap-uh-STRAH-noh
John of Damascus (Saint)	jon uhv duh-MAS-kuhs
John of Kanty (Saint)	jon uhv KAN-tee
John of the Cross (Saint)	jon uhv thuh KRAHS
John Paul (II, Saint)	jon pawl
John the Baptist (Saint)	jon thuh BAP-tist
Jonah	JOH-nuh
Jonam	JOH-nuhm
Joppa	JOP-uh
Joram	JOHR-uhm
Jordan	JOHR-d*n
Jorim	JOHR-ihm
Josaphat (Saint)	JOS-uh-fat
Joseph (Saint)	JOH-sihf or JOH-zuhf

Joseph Calasanz (Saint)	JOH-sihf or JOH-zuhf kal-uh-SAHNZ
Josephine Bakhita (Saint)	JOH-suh-feen bay-KEE-tuh or JOH-suh-feen bah-KEE-tuh
Joses	JOH-seez or JOH-sehz
Joshua	JOSH-oo-uh or JOSH-yoo-uh
Josiah	joh-SĪ-uh
Jotham	JOH-thuhm
Juan Diego Cuauhtlatoatzin (Saint)	hwan dee-AY-goh coo-oht-lah-TWAH-tzihn
jubilant	JOO-bih-luhnt
jubilation	joo-bih-LAY-shuhn
Jucal	JOO-kuhl
Judah	JOO-duh
Judaism	JOO-duh-ihz-*m or JOO-dee-ihz-*m
Judas	JOO-duhs
Jude (Saint)	jood
Judea	joo-DEE-uh or joo-DAY-uh
Junipero Serra (Saint)	hoo-NEE-pay-roh SER-uh
jurisdiction	jer-uhs-DIK-shuhn
justice	JUS-tuhs
justification	juhs-tuh-fih-KAY-shun
Justin (Saint)	JUS-tuhn
Justus	JUS-tuhs

K

Kadesh	KAY-dihsh
Kateri Tekakwitha (Saint)	kuh-TAYR-ee tehk-uh-WEE-tuh or KAY-tehr-ee tuh-KAK-wih-thuh
Katharine Drexel (Saint)	KATH-uh-rihn DREX-uhl
Kephas (Aramaic form of Cephas not used in the Lectionary but sometimes appears in commentaries.)	KEE-fuhs
Kerenhappuch	kehr-uhn-HAP-uhk
Kidron	KID-ruhn
kiln	kihln or kihl
kilometer	kih-LOM-uh-tehr
kilometre	kih-LOM-uh-tehr
Kings	kingz
Kiriatharba	kihr-ee-ath-AHR-buh
Kish	kish
knead	need
knee	nee

L

laborer	LAY-buhr-uhr
laden	LAY-d*n
lair	layr
laity	LAY-ih-tee
Lamech	LAY-mik
lament	luh-MENT
Lamentations	lam-ehn-TAY-shuhnz
Laodicea	lay-ahd-ih-SEE-uh
Lateran	LAT-ehr-uhn

latrine	la-TREEN
lattice	LAT-ihs
Lauda Sion	LAW-duh ZĪ-uhn or ZĪ-ahn
lava	LAH-vuh
lavish	LAV-ihsh
Lawrence (Saint)	LAHR-uhnz
Lawrence of Brindisi (Saint)	LAHR-uhnz uhv brihn-DEE-see or BRIN-dee-zee
Lawrence Ruiz (Saint)	LAHR-uhnz roo-EES or roo-EEZ
Lazarus (Saint)	LAZ-uh-ruhs
Leah	LEE-uh
leavened	LEV-uhnd
Lebanon	LEB-uh-nuhn
legion	LEE-juhn
legitimate	lih-JIT-uh-mit
Leo the Great (Saint)	LEE-oh
leper	LEP-ehr
leprosy	LEP-ruh-see
leprous	LEP-ruhs
Levi	LEE-vī
Levite	LEE-vīt
levitical	lih-VIT-ih-k*l
Leviticus	lih-VIT-ih-kuhs
liable	LI-uh-b*l
libations	li-BAY-shuhnz
Libya	LIB-ee-uh
licentious	lī-SEN-shuhs
lineage	LIN-ee-ihj

L

linen	LIN-uhn
lintel	LIN-t*l
liquor	LIK-ehr
loathe	loh<u>th</u>
loaves	lohvz
loincloths	LOYN-klawthz or LOYN-klawths
loins	loynz
Lois	LOH-ihs
Lord	lohrd
Lot	lot
Louis Mary de Montfort (Saint)	L<u>OO</u>-ee MAYR-ee d* MAHN-fert
Louis of France (Saint)	L<u>OO</u>-ihs or L<u>OO</u>-ee uhv frans
Louis-Zéphirin Moreau (Blessed)	l<u>oo</u>-EE zay-feer-AHN mohr-OH
Lourdes (Our Lady of)	loordz
Lucius	L<u>OO</u>-shee-uhs or L<u>OO</u>-shuhs
Lucy (Saint)	L<u>OO</u>-see
Lud	luhd
Luke (Saint)	l<u>oo</u>k
luminaries	L<u>OO</u>-mih-nayr-eez
lunatic	L<u>OO</u>-nuh-tihk
luxuriously	luhg-zhoor-ee-uhs-lee or luhk-shoor-ee-uhs-lee
Luz	l<u>oo</u>s or l<u>oo</u>z
Lycaonian	lihk-uh-OH-nee-uhn
Lydda	LID-uh
lyre	līr
Lysanias	lī-SAY-nee-uhs

Lysias	LIS-ee-uhs
Lystra	LIS-truh

M

Maccabees	MAK-uh-beez
mace	mays
Macedonia	mas-eh-DOH-nee-uh
Machpelah	mak-PEE-luh
Magdala	MAG-duh-luh
magistrate	MAJ-uh-strayt
magnificent	mag-NIF-uh-s*nt
Mahaluleel	muh-HAY-luh-lee-uhl
Malachi	MAL-uh-kī
Malchiah	mal-KĪ-uh
Malchus	MAL-kuhs
malefactor	MAL-uh-fak-ter
malice	MAL-ihs
malicious	muh-LISH-uhs
malign	muh-LĪN
maltreat	mal-TREET
mammon	MAM-uhn
Mamre	MAM-ree or MAHM-ray
Manaen	MAN-ee-uhn
Manasseh	muh-NAS-uh
manger	MAYN-jer
manifestation	man-ih-fes-TAY-shuhn
manna	MAN-uh
Manoah	mah-NOH-uh
mantle	MAN-t*l
manure	muh-NOOR or muh-NYOOR

maranatha	mar-uh-NATH-uh or mahr-uh-NATH-uh
marauder	muh-RAW-dehr
Marcellinus (Saint)	mar-suh-LĪ-nuhs
Margaret Mary Alacoque (Saint)	MAHR-guh-ruht MAYR-ee al-uh-KOHK
Margaret of Scotland (Saint)	MAHR-guh-ruht uhv SKAHT-luhnd
Marguerite Bourgeoys (Saint)	mahr-gehr-EET bohr-ZHWAH or mahr-gehr-EET bohr-ZHĪS
Marguerite d'Youville (Saint)	mahr-gehr-EET d* YOO-veel
Maguerite-Marie Alacoque	*See* Margaret Mary Alacoque
Mark (Saint)	mahrk
Maria Goretti (Saint)	muh-REE-uh guh-RET-ee
Marianne Cope (Saint)	mayr-ee-AN cohp
Marie de l'Incarnation	*See* Marie of the Incarnation
Marie of the Incarnation (Saint)	muh-REE uhv thee in-cahr-NAY-shuhn
Marie Rose Durocher (Blessed)	muh-REE rohz d*ROH-shehr or d*roh-SHAY
Marie-Anne Blondin (Blessed)	muh-ree AHN blahn-DUHN or muh-REE an BLON-duhn
Marie-Léonie Paradis (Blessed)	muh-REE lay-oh-NEE payr-uh-DEE
marr	mahr

marrow	MAYR-oh
Martha (Saint)	MAHR-thuh
Martin de Porres (Saint)	MAHR-t*n d* POHRS or MAHR-t*n day POHRS
Martin of Tours (Saint)	MAHR-t*n uhv toor
martyr	MAHR-tehr
Mary (Saint)	MAYR-ee
Mary Magdalene (Saint)	MAYR-ee MAG-duh-luhn or MAG-duh-leen
Mary Magdalene de' Pazzi (Saint)	MAYR-ee MAG-duh-leen day PAWT-zee or MAG-duh-luhn
Massah	MAS-uh
mastic	MAS-tihk
Mattan	MAT-uhn
Mattaniah	mat-uh-NĪ-uh
Mattatha	MAT-uh-thuh
Mattathias	mat-uh-THĪ-uhs
Matthan	MATH-uhn
Matthat	MATH-at
Matthew (Saint)	MATH-yoo
Matthias (Saint)	muh-THĪ-uhs
mature	muh-TYOOR or muh-TOOR or muh-CHOOR
Maximilian Mary Kolbe (Saint)	max-uh-MIL-yuhn MAYR-ee KOHL-bee
measure	ME-zhur
Medad	MEE-dad
Medes	meedz
media	MEE-dee-uh
mediator	MEE-dee-ay-tehr

Megiddo	meh-GID-doh
Melchi	MEL-chī
Melchizedek	mehl-KEEZ-uh-dehk or mehl-KIZ-uh-dehk
Melea	MEE-lee-uh
melodious	muh-LOH-dee-uhs
melon	MEL-uhn
mene	MEE-nee
Menna	MEN-uh
menstruous	MEN-stroo-uhs
merchant	MER-chuhnt
merciful	MER-sih-fuhl
Meribah	MAYR-ih-bah
Meshach	MEE-shak
Mesopotamia	mes-uh-poh-TAY-mee-uh
Messiah	meh-SĪ-uh
messianic	meh-see-AN-ihk
Methodius (Saint)	muh-THOH-dee-uhs
Methuselah	mih-THOO-suh-luh
Micah	MĪ-kuh
Micaiah	mih-KAY-yuh
Michael (Saint)	MĪ-k*l
Midian	MID-ee-uhn
Miguel Agustín Pro (Blessed)	mee-GEHL uh-goo-STEEN proh
Milcom	MIL-kuhm
Miletus	mī-LEE-tuhs
miraculous	mih-RAK-yoo-luhs
mirage	mih-RAHZH
mire	mīr
Miriam	MEER-ee-uhm

misery	MIZ-uhr-ee
mitre	MĪ-tehr
Moab	MOH-ab
Modein	MOH-deen
molten	MOHL-t*n
Monica (Saint)	MON-ih-kuh
moor	moor
Mordecai	MOHR-duh-kī
Moreh	MOHR-eh
Moriah	moh-RĪ-uh
mortar	MOHR-tuhr
mosaic	moh-ZAY-ihk
Moses	MOH-zihz or MOH-zihs
Moses'	MOH-zihz or MOH-zihs (not MOH-zihz-zihz)
Mosoch	MOH-sok
mourn	mohrn
Mount (as in Sinai)	mownt
mulberry	MUL-bayr-ee or MUL-buh-ree
multitude	MUL-tih-t<u>oo</u>d
mute	my<u>oo</u>t
mutton	MUH-tuhn
myriad	MEER-ee-uhd
myrrh	mer
Mysia	MIS-ee-uh

N

Naaman	NAY-uh-muhn
Naboth	NAY-both
Naggai	NAG-ī

Nahor	NAY-hohr
Nahshon	NAH-shon or NAH-shuhn
Nahum	NAY-huhm
Naim	naym
Nain	nayn
Naphtali	NAF-tuh-lī
nard	nahrd
Nathan	NAY-thuhn
Nathanael	nuh-THAN-ay-uhl
nativity	nuh-TIV-ih-tee
Nazarene	NAZ-uh-reen
Nazareth	NAZ-uh-rehth
nazirite	NAZ-uh-rīt
Nazorean	naz-uh-REE-uhn
Nebat	NEE-bat
Nebuchadnezzar	nehb-uh-kuhd-NEZ-uhr
Nebuzaradan	nehb-uh-zuh-RAY-duhn
necessity	nih-SES-uh-tee
Negeb	NEG-ehb
Nehemiah	nee-huh-MĪ-uh
Nehushta	nih-HOOSH-tuh or nuh-HOOSH-tuh
Ner	nuhr
Nereus (Saint)	NEE-rih-yoos
Neri	NEE-rī
nether	NETH-ehr
netherworld	NETH-ehr-wehrld
Nicanor	nī-KAY-nuhr
Nicholas (Saint)	NIK-oh-luhs
Nicholas of Antioch	NIK-oh-luhs uhv AN-tee-awk

Nicodemus	nihk-uh-DEE-muhs
Nicolaus	nihk-uh-LAY-uhs
Niger	$\text{N}\overline{\text{I}}$-guhr
Nile	$\text{n}\overline{\text{i}}\text{l}$
Nimshi	$\text{NIM-sh}\overline{\text{i}}$ or NIM-shee
Nineveh	NIN-uh-vuh
Ninevites	$\text{nihn-uh-V}\overline{\text{ITS}}$
Nisan	$\text{N}\overline{\text{I}}$-san
Noah	NOH-uh
Nola	NOH-luh
nonetheless	nuhn-thuh-LES
Norbert (Saint)	NOHR-behrt
nought	nawt
nullify	$\text{NUL-uh-f}\overline{\text{i}}$
numerous	NOO-mehr-uhs or NYOO-mehr-uhs
Nun	nuhn
nursling	NERS-lihng
Nykyta Budka (Blessed)	nih-KIT-uh BOOD-kuh

O

Obed	OH-bihd
oblation	oh-BLAY-shuhn
obliterate	uh-BLIT-uh-rayt or oh-BLIT-uh-rayt
obnoxious	ob-NOK-shuhs
obstinate	OB-stih-n*t
occupy	$\text{AWK-y}\underline{\text{oo}}\text{-p}\overline{\text{i}}$
offense	uh-FENTS
ointment	OYNT-muhnt
olives	OL-ihvz

Olivet	OL-ih-veht
Omega	oh-MAY-guh
Onesimus	oh-NES-uh-muhs or oh-NES-ih-muhs
Ophrah	OF-ruh
opportune	op-ehr-TOON or op-ehr-TYOON
oppress	oh-PRES
oracle	AWR-uh-kuhl or OHR-uh-kuhl
oracular	uh-RAK-yuh-lehr or oh-RAK-yuh-lehr
ordinance	OHR-d*n-uhns
orgy	OHR-jee
origin	OHR-ih-jihn
Orion	oh-RĪ-uhn
ornament	OHR-nuh-m*nt
orphan	OHR-fuhn
ostracize	OS-truh-sīz
oxen	AWK-zuhn

P

pagan	PAY-guhn
palace	PAL-uhs
Pamphylia	pam-FIL-ee-uh
Pancras (Saint)	PAN-kruhs
panel	PAN-uhl
Paphos	PAY-fos
parable	PAYR-uh-b*l
Paraclete	PAYR-uh-kleet
Paradise	PAYR-uh-dīs
paralytic	payr-uh-LIT-ihk

paralyzed	PAYR-uh-līzd
Paran	PAY-ruhn
parapet	PAYR-uh-puht or PAYR-uh-peht
Parath	PAY-ruhth
parentage	PAYR-uhn-t*j
pariah	puh-RĪ-uh
Parmenas	PAHR-muh-nuhs
Parthians	PAHR-thee-uhnz
partiality	pahr-shee-AL-uh-tee
paschal	PAS-kuhl
Pashhur	PASH-hehr
Passover	PAS-oh-vehr
pasture	PAS-chehr
paten	PA-tuhn
Patmos	PAT-muhs or PAT-mahs
patriarchs	PAY-tree-ahrks
Patrick (Saint)	PAT-rihk
Paul (Saint)	pawl
Paul Chŏng Hasang (Saint)	pawl chong HAH-sahng
Paul Miki (Saint)	pawl MEE-kee
Paul of the Cross (Saint)	pawl uhv thuh krahs
Paulinus of Nola (Saint)	paw-LĪ-nuhs uhv NOH-luh
peculiarly	peh-KEWL-yuhr-lee
Pekah	PEE-kuh
Peleg	PEE-lihg
Peñafort	PEN-yuh-fohr
penance	PEN-uhnts
pendant	PEN-d*nt

Peniel	PEN-ee-uhl
Peninnah	pih-NIN-uh
Pentecost	PEN-tih-kost
perceive	per-SEEV
perdure	per-DYOOR
peres	PEE-rehs
Perez	PEE-rihz or PAYR-ez
Perga	PER-guh
Pergamum	PER-guh-muhm
perish	PAYR-ihsh
perishable	PAYR-ihsh-uh-b*l
Perizzites	PAYR-ihsh-zīts
perjury	PER-juh-ree
Perpetua (Saint)	pehr-PET-choo-uh or pehr-PET-oo-uh
perpetual	pehr-PECH-oo-uhl
persecute	PER-suh-kyoot
persecution	pehr-suh-KYOO-shuhn
perseverance	pehr-suh-VEER-uhns
persevere	pehr-suh-VEER
Persia	PER-zhuh
persistence	pehr-SIS-t*ns
persistent	pehr-SIS-t*nt
perturbed	pehr-TERBD
perverse	pehr-VERS
pestilence	PES-tuh-luhnts
Peter (Saint)	PEE-tehr
Peter Canisius (Saint)	PEE-tehr kuh-NEE-see-uhs or kuh-NIHSH-ee-uhs
Peter Chanel (Saint)	PEE-tehr shuh-NEL
Peter Chrysologus (Saint)	PEE-tehr kris-OL-uh-guhs

Peter Claver (Saint)	PEE-tehr KLAY-vehr
Peter Damian (Saint)	PEE-tehr DAY-mee-uhn
Peter Julian Eymard (Saint)	PEE-tehr JOO-lee-uhn AY-mar
Phanuel	FAN-yoo-ehl or fuh-NYOO-uhl
Pharaoh	FAYR-oh
Pharisees	FAYR-uh-seez
Philadelphia	fihl-uh-DEL-fee-uh
Philemon	fī-LEE-muhn
Philip (Saint)	FIL-ihp
Philip Neri (Saint)	FIL-ihp NEER-ee
Philippi	fih-LIP-ī
Philippians	fih-LIP-ee-uhnz
Philistia	fih-LIS-tee-uh
Philistine	fih-LIS-teen
philosophy	fih-LAHS-uh-fee
Phinehas	FIN-ee-huhs
Phoenicia	fuh-NEE-shuh or fih-NISH-uh
Phrygia	FRIJ-ee-uh
phylacteries	fih-LAK-tuh-reez
piety	PĪ-uh-tee
pigeon	PI-juhn
Pi-hahiroth	pī-huh-HĪ-roth
Pilate	PĪ-luht
pilgrimage	PIL-gruh-mihj
pillar	PI-luhr
pinnacle	PIN-uh-k*l
Pisidia	pih-SID-ee-uh
Pithom	PĪ-thom

Pithon	PĪ-thon
pitiable	PIT-ee-uh-b*l
Pius (V and X, Saint)	PĪ-uhs
Pius of Pietrelcina (Saint)	PĪ-uhs uhv pee-ay-trehl-CHEE-nuh
pivots	PIV-uhts
plague	playg
plaintive	PLAYN-tihv
plateau	pla-TOH
Pleiades	PLEE-uh-deez
plenteous	PLEN-tyuhs
plentiful	PLEN-tih-fuhl
ploughshares	PLOW-shayrz
pollute	puh-L<u>OO</u>T
Polycarp (Saint)	POL-ee-kahrp
Pontian (Saint)	PON-tee-uhn
Pontius	PON-shuhs
Pontus	PON-tuhs
portent	POHR-tent
portico	POHR-tih-koh
portion	POHR-shuhn
position	poh-ZIH-shuhn
possess	poh-ZESS
posterity	pos-TAYR-ih-tee
praetorium	prih-TOHR-ee-uhm
precept	PREE-sehpt
precincts	PREE-sihngkts
precious	PRESH-uhs
prediction	prih-DIK-shuhn
preeminent	pree-EHM-ih-nuhnt

prefer	prih-FUHR
presbyters	PREZ-bih-ters
prescribe	prih-SKRĪB
presence	PREZ-uhnts
presentable	prih-ZEN-tuh-b*l
preserve	prih-ZERV
prestige	prehs-TEEJ
pretentious	pree-TEN-shuhs
pretext	PREE-tehkst
prey	pray
primacy	PRĪ-muh-see
principalities	prihn-suh-PAL-uh-teez
Prisca	PRIS-kuh
proceed (verb)	proh-SEED
proceeds (noun)	PROH-seedz
Prochorus	PRAH-kuh-ruhs
proclaim	proh-KLAYM
proconsul	proh-KAHN-suhl
procreation	proh-cree-AY-shuhn
procurator	PROK-yuh-ray-tehr
prodigy	PROD-uh-jee
produce (verb)	proh-D<u>OO</u>S
profanation	prah-fuh-NAY-shuhn
profane	proh-FAYN
proficient	proh-FISH-uhnt
profitable	PROF-iht-uh-b*l
profulgence	proh-FUHL-j*ns
progeny	PRAH-juh-nee
progress (verb)	pruh-GRES
progress (noun)	PRAH-grehs

prophecy (noun)	PROF-uh-see
prophesy (verb)	PROF-uh-sī
prophet	PRAH-fuht
prophetic	pruh-FET-ihk
propriety	pruh-PRĪ-uh-tee
proscribe	proh-SKRĪB
prosperity	pros-PAYR-uh-tee
prostitute	PROS-tuh-t<u>oo</u>t or PROS-tuh-ty<u>oo</u>t
prostrate	PROS-trayt
Proverbs	PRAH-verbz
prudent	PR<u>OO</u>-duhnt
Psalms	sawlmz or sahmz
psaltery	SAWL-tuh-ree
puberty	PY<u>OO</u>-buhr-tee
purge	perj
purification	pyoor-ih-fih-KAY-shuhn
purifier	PYOOR-uh-fī-*r
pursue	per-S<u>OO</u>
pustule	PUHS-chool or PUHS-tyool
Put	poot
Puteoloi	py<u>oo</u>-TEE-oh-lee

Q

Qoheleth	koh-HEL-uhth
qorban	KOHR-buhn
Quartus	KWOHR-tuhs
Quirinius	kwih-RIN-ee-uhs
quiver	KWI-vehr

R

Raamses	ray-AM-seez
Rabbah	RAB-uh
Rabbi	RAB-ī
Rabboni	rab-OH-nee
Rabbouni	rab-OO-nī
Rachel	RAY-chuhl
radiant	RAY-dee-uhnt
Raguel	ruh-GYOO-uhl
Rahab	RAY-hab
Ram	ram
Ramah	RAY-muh
Ramathaim	ram-uh-THAY-im
ransomed	RAN-suhmd
Raphael (Saint)	RAH-fī-ehl or RAY-fī-ehl
Raqa	RAH-kah
ration	RASH-uhn or RAY-shuhn
ravenous	RAV-ih-nuhs
ravine	ruh-VEEN
Raymond of Peñafort (Saint)	RAY-muhnd uhv PEN-yuh-fohr or RAY-muhnd uhv PEN-uh-fohr
razor	RAY-zuhr
realization	ree-uh-luh-ZAY-shuhn
rebel (verb)	rih-BEL
rebuke	rih-BYOOK
recognize	REC-uhg-nīz
recompense	REK-uhm-pens
reconcile	REK-uhn-sīl
reconciliation	rek-uhn-sihl-ee-AY-shuhn

recourse	REE-kohrs
recumbent	rih-KUM-b*nt
refuge	REF-yooj
refulgence	rih-FUHL-j*nts
refuse (noun)	REF-yoos
refuse (verb)	rih-FYOOZ
Rehoboam	ree-huh-BOH-uhm
reign	rayn
rein	rayn
rekindle	ree-KIN-d*l
reliable	rih-LĪ-uh-b*l
remedy	REM-uh-dee
remembrance	rih-MEM-bruhns
remnant	REM-n*nt
remonstrate	REM-*n-strayt
renown	rih-NOWN
repast	rih-PAST
repentance	rih-PEN-t*ns
repentant	rih-PEN-t*nt
Rephidim	REF-ih-dim
reprimand	REP-ruh-mand
reproach	rih-PROHCH
reproof	rih-PROOF
reprove	rih-PROOV
reputable	REP-yuh-tuh-b*l
reputation	rep-yoo-TAY-shuhn
require	ree-KWĪR
resin	REZ-*n
respectable	rih-SPEK-tuh-b*l
resplendent	rih-SPLEN-d*nt

resurrection	rez-uh-REK-shuhn
retinue	RET-*n-oo or RET-*n-yoo
retribution	reh-truh-BYOO-shuhn
Reu	REE-yoo
Reuben	ROO-bin
Revelation	rehv-uh-LAY-shuhn
revelry	REV-uhl-ree
revere	reh-VEER
revile	rih-VĪL
revolutionary	reh-voh-LOO-shun-ayr-ee
Rhegium	REE-jee-uhm
Rhesa	REE-suh
Rezin	REE-zihn
Riblah	RIB-luh
ridicule	RID-uh-kyool
righteous	RĪ-chuhs
Robert Bellarmine (Saint)	RAH-bert BEL-uhr-meen
rogue	rohg
Romans	ROH-muhnz
Rome	rohm
Romuald (Saint)	ROM-yoo-uhl*d
rosary	ROH-suh-ree
Rose of Lima (Saint)	rohz uhv LEE-muh
Rose Philippine Duchesne (Saint)	rohz fihl-ih-PEEN doo-KAYN
rouse	rowz
route	root or rowt
ruddy	RUHD-ee
Rufus	ROO-fuhs
rumor	ROO-muhr
Ruth	rooth

S

Sabbath	SAB-uhth
sacred	SAY-krehd
sacrificial	sak-ruh-FISH-uhl
Sadducees	SAD-yoo-seez
Sala	SAY-luh
Salamis	SAL-uh-mihs
Salathiel	suh-LAY-thee-uhl
Salem	SAY-luhm
Salim	SAY-lim
saliva	suh-LĪ-vuh
Salmon	SAL-muhn
Salome	suh-LOH-mee
Salu	SAY-loo
salutation	sal-yoo-TAY-shun
salvation	sal-VAY-shuhn
salves	savz
Samaria	suh-MAYR-ee-uh
Samaritan	suh-MAYR-uh-tuhn
Samson	SAM-suhn
Samuel	SAM-yoo-uhl
sanctification	sangk-tuh-fih-KAY-shuhn
sanctify	SANGK-tih-fī
sanctuary	SANGK-choo-ayr-ee
Sanhedrin	san-HEE-druhn
sapphire	SAF-īr
Sarah	SAYR-uh
Sarai	SAYR-ī
Saraph	SAYR-uhf
Saraphat	SAYR-uh-fat

Sarasadai	sayr-uh-SAD-ī
Sardis	SAHR-dihs
Satan	SAY-t*n
Saul	sawl
Savior	SAYV-yehr
scabbard	SCA-b*rd
scepter	SEP-tehr
sceptre	SEP-tehr
Scholastica (Saint)	skoh-LAS-tih-kuh
sciatic	sī-A-tihk
scimitar	SIM-ih-tahr
scoff	skof or skawf
scorpion	SKOHR-pee-uhn
scourge	skerj
scribe	skrīb
scripture	SKRIP-chehr
scrutiny	SKR<u>OO</u>-tih-nee
Scythian	SITH-ee-uhn
seah	SEE-ah
searing	SEER-ing
seavors	SEE-vehrz
Seba	SEE-buh
Sebastian (Saint)	suh-BAS-tee-uhn
seclusion	sih-KLOO-zhuhn
securely	suh-KYUHR-lee
seductive	sih-DUHK-tihv
Seir	SEE-uhr
seize	seez
semblance	SEM-bl*ns
Semein	SEM-ee-uhn

Sennacherib	suh-NAK-uh-rihb
senses	SEN-s*z
sensual	SEN-shoo-uhl
sensuality	sehn-shoo-AL-uh-tee
sentinel	SEN-tih-nuhl
separate	SEP-uh-ruht
sequence	SEE-kwentz
seraph	SAYR-uhf
seraphim	SAYR-uh-fihm
serpent	SER-p*nt
Serug	SEER-uhg
Seruy	SUH-ree
Servites (Order of)	SER-vīts
Seth	seth
Shaalim	SHAY-uh-lihm
Shadrach	SHAD-rak
shaken	SHAY-k*n
Shalishah	shuh-LĪ-shuh
Shalmaneser	shal-muh-NEE-zuhr
shamefacedly	SHAYM-fay-sid-lee
Shammah	SHAM-uh
Shaphan	SHAY-fuhn
Shaphat	SHAY-fat
Sharbel Makhlūf (Saint)	SHAHR-b*l mahk-LOOF
Sharon	SHAYR-uhn
sheaf	sheef
Shealtiel	shee-AL-tee-uhl
Shear-jashub	SHEE-uhr-jay-shuhb
Sheba	SHEE-buh
Shebna	SHEB-nah

Shechem	SHEK-uhm
shekel	SHEK-*l
Shelah	SHEE-luh
Shelemiah	shehl-uh-MĪ-uh
Shem	shem
Sheol	SHAY-ohl or SHEE-ohl
Shephatiah	shef-uh-TĪ-uh
Shiloh	SHĪ-loh
Shilonite	SHĪ-luh-nīt
Shimei	SHIM-ee-ī
Shinar	SHĪ-nahr or SHEE-nahr
shining	SHĪ-ning
shriek	shreek
Shunem	SHOO-nuhm
Shunummite	SHOO-nuh-mīt
Shur	shoor
Sidon	SĪ-duhn
Sidonian	si-DOH-nee-uhm
siege	seezh
Siena	see-EN-uh
sieve	siv
sigh	sī
Silas	SĪ-luhs
Siloam	sih-LOH-uhm
Silvanus	sihl-VAY-nuhs
Simeon	SIM-ee-uhn
similarly	SIM-ih-luhr-lee
Simon	SĪ-muhn
Simon (Saint)	SĪ-muhn
Simon de Montfort (Saint)	SĪ-muhn duh MAHNT-fehrt

Sinai	SĪ-nī
sinew	SIN-y<u>oo</u>
Sirach	SEER-ak or SĪ-ruhk
sistrum	SIS-truhm
Sixtus (Saint)	SIKS-tuhs
slaughter	SLAW-tehr
Smyrna	SMER-nuh
snare	snayr
Sodom	SOD-uhm
sojourn	SOH-jehrn
solemnity	suh-LEM-nuh-tee
solicitude	suh-LIS-uh-tood or suh-LIS-uh-tyood
Solomon	SOL-uh-muhn
sores	sohrs
Sosthenes	SOS-thuh-neez
sovereign	SOV-ehr-uhn or SOV-ruhn
sovereignty	SOV-ehr-uhn-tee or SOV-ruhn-tee
spectacle	SPEK-tuh-k*l
splendor	SPLEN-duhr
spore	spohr
squander	SKWAHN-dehr
Stabat Mater	STAH-baht MAH-tehr
Stanislaus (Saint)	STAN-ihs-lahs
stature	STACH-ehr
statute	STACH-<u>oo</u>t
steadfast	STED-fast
stealth	stelth
Stephen (Saint)	STEE-vuhn

Stephen of Hungary	STEE-vuhn uhv HUNG-uh-ree
steppe	step
steward	ST<u>OO</u>-erd or STY<u>OO</u>-ehrd
strangle	STRAN-guhl
stupefied	ST<u>OO</u>-puh-fīd
styles	stīlz
sublime	suh-BLĪM
sublimity	suhb-LIM-ih-tee
Succoth	SUHK-uhth
sullied	SUH-leed
sulpherous	SUHL-fer-uhs
summon	SUHM-uhn
sumptuous	SUMP-ch<u>oo</u>-uhs
supplication	sup-lih-KAY-shuhn
surveillance	sehr-VAY-l*ns
Susanna	s<u>oo</u>-ZAN-uh
suspense	suh-SPENTS
sustain	suh-STAYN
swaddling	SWAHD-lihng
sword	sohrd
sycamore	SIK-uh-mohr
Sychar	SĪ-kahr or SIH-kahr or sih-KAHR
Syene	sī-EE-nee
Sylvester (Saint)	sihl-VES-tehr
Symeon	SIM-ee-uhn
sympathy	SIM-puh-thee
synagogue	SIN-uh-gog
synod	SIH-nuhd
Syracuse	SEER-uh-ky<u>oo</u>z

Syria	SEER-ee-uh
Syrophoenician	sī-roh-fuh-NEE-shuhn

T

Tabeel	TAB-ee-uhl
Tabernacles	TAB-uhr-nak-*lz
Tabitha	TAB-ih-thuh
talents	TAL-untz
Talitha cum	tal-uh-thuh KOOM or tah-lee-thah KOOM
Talitha cumi	tal-uh-thuh KOO-mī or tah-lee-thah KOO-mī
Talitha koum	tal-uh-thuh KOOM or tah-lee-thah KOOM
Tamar	TAY-mahr
tambourine	tam-buh-REEN
tarry	TAYR-ee
Tarshish	TAHR-shihsh
Tarsus	TAHR-suhs
tassel	TASS-*l
taunt	tawnt
Te Deum	tay-DAY-uhm
Tekel	TEK-uhl
temerity	tuh-MER-uh-tee
temperately	TEM-pehr-iht-lee
tempest	TEM-pihst
tenant	TEN-*nt
Terah	TER-uh
terebinth	TAYR-uh-binth
Teresa of Jesus (Saint)	teh-RAY-suh or tuh-REE-suh
terrify	TAYR-ih-fī

testify	TES-tuh-fī
testimony	TES-tuh-moh-nee
tethered	TE<u>TH</u>-*rd
tetrarch	TET-rahrk
Thaddaeus	THAD-ee-uhs
Thau	tow
the (before consonants, as in "The word [Gospel] of the Lord.")	<u>th</u>uh
the (before vowels, as in "The Acts of the Apostles")	<u>th</u>ee
Theophilus	thee-AWF-uh-luhs
Thérèse of the Child Jesus (Saint)	teh-REZ
Thessalonians	thes-uh-LOH-nee-uhnz
thicket	THIK-iht
thistle	THIS-uhl
Thomas	TOM-uhs
Thomas Aquinas (Saint)	TOM-uhs uh-KWĪ-nuhs
Thomas Becket (Saint)	TOM-uhs BEK-uht
Thomas More (Saint)	TOM-uhs mohr
thorough	THER-oh
thousandth	THOW-z*nth or THOW-z*ndth
threshold	THRESH-ohld or THRESH-hohld
Thyatir	thī-uh-TĪ-ruh
Tiberias	tī-BEER-ee-uhs
Tiberius	tī-BEER-ee-uhs
Timaeus	tī-MEE-uhs or tih-MAY-uhs
timbrel	TIM-brehl

Timon	TĪ-muhn
Timothy (Saint)	TIM-uh-thee
Tishbe	TISH-bee
Tishbite	TISH-bīt
tithe	tiṯẖ
Titus (Saint)	TĪ-tuhs
Tobit	TOH-biht
token	TOH-kuhn
tolerable	TOL-ehr-uh-b*l
tongs	tawngs
tongues	tuhngs
Toribio de Mogrovejo (Saint)	toḥ-REE-bee-oh day moh-groh-VEY-ho
torrent	TOHR-*nt
torture	TOHR-chehr
Trachonitis	trak-uh-NĪ-tihs
Transfiguration	trans-fihg-yehr-AY-shun
transfigure	trans-FIG-yehr
transgress	trans-GRES or tranz-GRES
transgression	trans-GRESH-uhn or tranz-GRESH-uhn
trepidation	trehp-uh-DAY-shuhn
trespass	TRES-puhs or TRES-pas
tribulation	trih-byoo-LAY-shuhn
tribunal	trī-BYOO-n*l or trih-BYOO-n*l
tribute	trih-BYOOT
Triduum	TRID-oo-uhm
Trinity	TRIN-ih-tee
Troas	TROH-az

Tubal	TOO-buhl
tunic	TOO-nihk
Tychicus	TIK-uh-kuhs
tyrannical	tih-RAN-ih-kuhl
tyrant	TĪ-ruhnt
Tyre	tīr
Tyrian	TEER-ee-uhn

U

unabated	uhn-uh-BAY-t*d
unaltered	uhn-AHL-tehrd-uh-b*l
unanimously	yoo-NAN-uh-muhs-lee
unapproachable	uhn-uh-PROH-chuh-b*l
uncircumcision	uhn-sehr-kuhm-SIH-zhuhn
unduly	uhn-DOO-lee or uhn-DYOO-lee
unimpeded	uhn-ihm-PEED-*d
uninhabited	uhn-ihn-HAB-uh-t*d
unity	YOO-nih-tee
unleavened	uhn-LEV-uhnd
unmerciful	uhn-MER-sih-fuhl
unreservedly	uhn-rih-ZERV-uhd-lee
unruly	uhn-ROO-lee
untie	uhn-TĪ
upright	UHP-rīt
Ur	oor
Urbanus	uhr-BAY-nuhs
Uriah	yoo-RĪ-uh
usury	YOO-suh-ree
utensils	yoo-TEN-sihlz

utterance	UHT-ehr-*ns
utters	UH-tehrz
Uzziah	uh-ZĪ-uh

V

valid	VAL-ihd
vanity	VAN-ih-tee
various	VAYR-ee-uhs
Vasyl Velychkowsky (Blessed)	vah-SIL vihl-ihch-KOHV-skee
vehement	VEE-uh-m*nt
veil	vayl
vengeance	VEN-j*ns
Veni sancte spiritus	VAY-nee SAHNG-tay SPEER-ee-t<u>oo</u>s
Vercelli	vuhr-CHEL-ee
verdant	VER-duhnt
verify	VAYR-ih-fī
vestibule	VES-tuh-by<u>oo</u>l
vexation	vehk-SAY-shuhn
Vianney	vee-AH-nee
Viaticum	vī-AT-ih-kuhm or vee-AT-ih-kuhm
Victimae paschali laudes	VEEK-tee-may pah-SKAH-lee LAH-days
vigilant	VIJ-ihl-uhnt
Vincent (Saint)	VIN-sihnt
Vincent de Paul (Saint)	VIN-sihnt d* PAHL
Vincent Ferrer (Saint)	VIN-sihnt fuh-RAYR
vindication	vihn-dih-KAY-shuhn
vineyard	VIN-yehrd

vintage	VIN-tihj
violation	vī-oh-LAY-shuhn
virtue	VER-ch<u>oo</u>
visible	VIZ-uh-b*l
Visitation	viz-ih-TAY-shuhn
vocation	voh-KAY-shuhn
vulture	VUHL-chuhr

W

wadi	WAH-dee
wail	way<u>l</u>
wanton	WAHN-tuhn
warrior	WAHR-ee-uhr
waver	WAY-vehr
wayfarer	WAY-fayr-uhr
weaned	weend
Wenceslaus (Saint)	WEN-suhs-lahs
whelm	hwelm
whelp	hwelp
whomever	h<u>oo</u>m-EV-uhr
wicked	WIK-uhd
widow	WID-oh
windings	WĪN-dihngz
winged	wingd or WING-uhd
winnowing	WIN-oh-wihng
Wisdom	WIZ-duhm
wither	WI<u>TH</u>-ehr
wolves	wuhlvz
womb	w<u>oo</u>m
wondrous	WUHN-druhs
worship	WER-shihp

wrath	rath
wretch	retch
wrought	rot

X

Xavier (Saint)	ZAY-vee-uhr

Y

Yahweh	YAH-way
Yahweh-yireh	YAH-way-YEER-ay
yield	yeeld
yoke	yohk
yolk	yohk

Z

Zacchaeus	zuh-KEE-uhs
Zadok	ZAD-uhk or ZAY-dok
Zarephath	ZAYR-uh-fath
zeal	zeel
Zealot	ZEL-uht
zealous	ZEL-uhs
Zebedee	ZEB-uh-dee
Zeboiim	zuh-BOY-ihm
Zebulun	ZEB-yoo-luhn
Zechariah	zek-uh-RĪ-uh
Zedekiah	zed-uh-KĪ-uh
Zephaniah	zef-uh-NĪ-uh
Zerah	ZEER-uh
Zeror	ZEER-ohr
Zerubbabel	zuh-ROOB-uh-b*l
Zeruiah	zuh-ROO-uh

Zeus	z<u>oo</u>s
Ziklag	ZIK-lag
Zion	ZĪ-uhn or ZĪ-ahn
Ziph	zif
Zorah	ZOHR-uh
Zuph	zuhf